WHAT TO DO
With The
NEW YOU

By DICK LOWEY

xulon
PRESS

Copyright © 2014 By Dick Lowey

What To Do With The New You

by By Dick Lowey

Printed in the United States of America

ISBN 9781498417235

All rights reserved solely by the author. The author guarantees all contents are original and do not infringe upon the legal rights of any other person or work. No part of this book may be reproduced in any form without the permission of the author. The views expressed in this book are not necessarily those of the publisher.

Scripture quotations taken from the New King James Version (NKJV). Copyright © 1979, 1980, 1982 by Thomas Nelson, Inc. Used by permission. All rights reserved.

www.xulonpress.com

TABLE OF CONTENTS

1. Getting the Gospel Right – (P's and S's) 15
2. Who Do You Think You Are?
   (20 Truths Regarding the New You) 18
3. The Two Levels of Salvation 41
4. His Story and My Story. 59
5. Two Foundational Scripture Verses 66
6. The Three-Legged Stool – (Word, Prayer,
   Fellowship) 68
7. Time Alone with God – ("Quiet Time"–
   Devotions). 70
8. Speaking to the Mountain 75
9. Your Forever Family – (The Church) 78
10. The 4 Wills of God – (Dilemma/Solution) . . . 81

DEDICATION

Inspired by Philip Darby McDonald

Dedicated to Gary Willard Downing

ACKNOWLEDGEMENTS

This book comes out of the years of Bible studies I taught in Pennsylvania, Illinois, and Minnesota when I was on the staff of Young Life. I would like to thank the following people for their encouragement and help: my wonderful and esteemed associates- Cindy Shepherd and Paul Kaufman {who worked five twelve hour days writing and rewriting this material when I came to Phoenix, Ax. Crying out to them after labor day- 2014} Also, John Sanny who encouraged me to complete the book.] Tom Klein, who supplied me with "loweyisms" he had been keeping for years!, Bud Anderson, my forever pal in the Lord, Rob Lineer, faithful leader of leaders, Patty Hardy White- and Kathy Downing- who further encouraged me. Also, thanks to Tony Ducklow, Reed Austin, Gail Berger, the Trosen family, Dick Hamblin, Gordy Nagel, Alan Ploetz, Pastor Jeff Jarvis, and so many other from Christ Community Church, Hope Presbyterian Church, Christ Presbyterian Church. Last- but not least- a fervent thanks to Joan McDonald {Phil McDonald's wife} and my "best girl" encourager – Ingeborg Gates

INTRODUCTION

A note to teachers:

The first and primary need of the new believer is — relationship with a mature mentor. Jesus knew that understanding of the New Covenant was "caught" as much as it was "taught". Therefore, it is of utmost importance that the leaders spend "life-affirming time" with the "new ones".

Let me share an accrostic that has helped leaders in the past. It spells:

LOVE

L — Let the other person be the way they are
O — Open yourself up to that person
V — Verbalize your appreciation for that person
E — Encourage that other person

Question

Some of you may be wondering if you are qualified to lead these young ones in the faith. How do you help them pursue their new life in Christ? After all, you may be just beginning to apply scripture to your own life. You may not have been to seminary. Perhaps you've only been a believer a few years...

Or, maybe you've walked with Christ for along time but struggle with mentoring someone new to the faith.

So you wonder, "are you qualified?" The answer is probably NO!

But wait a minute, what if the approach called for is not so much "teaching them" but "learning **with** them"? What I like to call "mutual exploration". Now things are on a different basis. You are qualified to lead discussions and even draw conclusions (summarize) at appropriate times and (with God's Word in front of you and The Holy Spirit in you) you can trust that God gave you these "new ones" to care fore and He will give you whatever you need in serving them!

Philippians 4:13 says: *"I can do ALL things through Christ who strengthens me!"* So be confident in Him and let the Spirit lead... Learn together.

Chapter 1

CHRIST-THE BIBLE'S MESSAGE

The Biblical message is CHRIST!
In the Apostle Paul's letter to the Galatians, he asked the new believers the following question: Did you get the right Gospel-"Good News" Message? This is crucially important, because it is foundational. He writes, *"I marvel that you are turning away so soon from Him who called you in the Grace of Christ to a different Gospel, which is not another; but there are some who trouble you and want to pervert the Gospel of Christ. But even if we, or an angel from heaven preach any other Gospel to you than what we have preached to you, let him be damned!"* Galatians 1:1-9

The Apostle Paul summarizes the accurate Gospel in 1 Corinthians 15:1-7. Read through this passage. It can easily be memorized with the following acrostics using the letters "S" and "P":

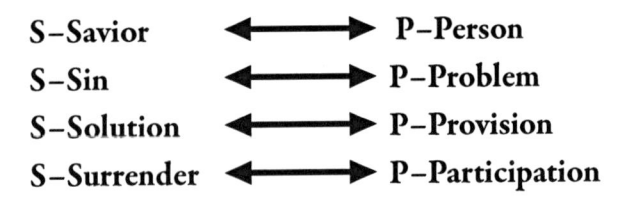

S–Savior ⟷ P–Person
S–Sin ⟷ P–Problem
S–Solution ⟷ P–Provision
S–Surrender ⟷ P–Participation

A little explanation may be helpful here:
Savior and **Person** are one in the same: Jesus, the Christ
The **Problem** of **Sin** is what separates us from God
Christ **Provides** the **Solution**–by dying in our place
Our appropriate response is to **Surrender** to God and
Participate by being ready to do God's will.

Many have found it helpful to recite these lists out loud several times–maybe at the end of each Bible Study session.

The basic message of Paul's letter to the Galatians is: **Don't even think about adding the Law (The Ten Commandments) to the Gospel of Grace!**

The Gospel is: Jesus Christ
His death and resurrection
plus nothing.
Jesus paid it all — He said: "IT IS FINISHED !"
So just accept it.

P.S.

I heard the famous theologian, Paul Tillich, lecture back in 1963 at Northwestern University, and during the Q. and A. time, a graduate student asked him for a simple definition of a Christian.

Without hesitation, Tillich replied: "Christians are those who have accepted the fact that they are accepted !"

Wow !

Our sins — Past — Present — and **<u>Future</u>** — are forgiven and forgotten by our Lord who paid the full price for them ALL.

(In the above sentence, I've bolded and underlined the word "future" because this is the one we forget or find difficult to believe.)

Romans 8:1 says it so clearly: *"There is therefore now no condemnation to those who are in Christ Jesus!"*

Chapter 2

WHO DO YOU THINK YOU ARE?

20 TRUTHS REGARDING THE NEW YOU

Scripture makes it very clear that God wants you to see yourself as the "NEW YOU" — As a new person in Christ.

We're told in 2 Corinthians 5:17: *"Therefore if anyone is in Christ, he is a new creation, old things have passed away, behold, all things have become new!"*

I can identify in Scripture twenty truths (gifts of Grace) that each of us received permanently and eternally when we accepted Christ into our lives for salvation. These truths are now YOURS to claim and to live by.

NOTE:
The key verses are written out. You are encouraged to look up and ponder the others listed.

TRUTH # 1: YOU WERE PUT INTO GOD'S PLAN ETERNALLY

Jeremiah 29:11: *"For I know the thoughts that I think towards you, says the Lord. Thoughts of peace and not of evil, to give you a future and a hope..."*

("Thoughts" is a key word here: *"Machashabeth"* in Hebrew means: Plans, Intentions, Thoughts, Purposes, Directions, Assignments, Uses.)

So, God planned the best for you!

A. You were foreknown by God

This means God knew all about you before you were born! He knew all about your sins and weaknesses and decided to love you and save you in spite of it all — so praise Him and thank Him often!

In Romans 8:28-30 we read: *"And we know that all things work together for good to those who love God, to those who are the called according to His purpose. For whom He foreknew, He also predestined to be conformed to the image of His Son, that He might be the firstborn among many brothers. Moreover whom He predestined, these He also called, whom He called, these He also justified, and who He jistified, these He also glorified."*

Read and think about: Acts 2:23
                        1 Peter 1:2

B. You are one of the "elect" — chosen by God

"Who shall bring a charge against God's elect?"
Romans 8:33

C. You were predestined
Predestined means "pre-planned for". This doesn't cancel free will because His choice of you is based in His forknowledge of your decision for Him. Look again at Romans 8: 29 & 30.

TRUTH # 2: YOU WERE RECONCILED
A. By God
"Now all things are of God, <u>who has reconciled us to Himself through Jesus Christ</u>, and has given us the ministry of reconciliation that is, that God was in Christ reconciling the world to himself, not imputing their trespasses to them, and has connitted to us the work of reconciliation." 2 Corinthians 5:18 & 19

ACTIVE ILLUSTRATION
Imagine someone coming up in front of you with his back turned to you and you turn your back to him, so that you're both facing in opposite directions. At this point you announce that because of Jesus' cross and resurrection, God has freed Himself from condemning the human race and can now love them. You therefore turn around towards the back of the other person. Then ask: "What is left to happen so that reconciliation can take place?"

Read and talk about Colossians 1: 20 and 2 Corinthians 5:20.

B. To God
"For if, when we were His enemies, <u>we were reconciled to God</u> through the death of His Son... much more having been reconciled, we shall be saved by His life!" Romans 5:10

(We are saved — given constant victory — by His life in us by The Holy Spirit.)

Look also at Ephesians 2:14-17

TRUTH #3: YOU WERE PURCHASED (REDEEMED) WITH THE FULL PRICE PAID BY GOD
Ephesians 1:7&8: *<u>"In Him we have redemption through His blood,</u> the forgiveness of sins, according to the riches of His Grace which He made to abound toward us in all wisdom and prudence..."*
Or from our "earliest Gospel" — Job 19:25: *"I know that my redeemer* (the One who pays the full price) *lives, and He shall stand at last* (in a future time) *on the earth..."*
Read also: Romans 3:23&24, Colossians 1:14 and 1 Peter 1:18.

TRUTH # 4: NO MORE CONDEMNATION
"There is therefore, now <u>no condemnation</u> to those who are in Christ Jesus." Romans 8:1

Read also John 3:18

TRUTH # 5: PROPITIATION

Through Christ's death on the cross, God's demand for justice is accomplished. God's justice (His righteous anger towards that which will destroy us) is satisfied.

God's wrath against sin — (our rebellious bond with "self-destruction") has been poured out on Christ at the cross.

The Old Testament prophet, Isaiah, writes: *"All we like sheep have gone astray... we have turned, every one, to his own way... and the Lord has laid on Him the iniquity of us all."* Isaiah 53:6

Read and reflect also upon: Romans 3:24- 26 and 1 John 2:2

TRUTH # 6: YOU HAVE BEEN GIVEN NEW BIRTH

In John 3:7 Jesus said, *"Do not mavel that I said to you, 'you must be born again...'"*

And as a result of that new birth we're told in 1 Peter 1:23 that we are now God's children.

The Gospel of John expresses the same idea in John 1:12 where we read: *"But as many as received Him, to them He gave the right to become the children of God...to those who believe in His Name."*

See also Galatians 3:26, 1 John 3:2

Because of our new birth, along with becoming the children of God, we are also told we are "a new creation": *"For in Christ Jesus neither circumcision or uncircumcision avails anything but a <u>new creation</u>..."* Galations 6:15

See also: Ephesians 2:10 and 2 Corinthians 5:17

TRUTH # 7: YOU'VE BEEN ADOPTED INTO GOD'S FAMILY

NOTE: The thing an adopted child needs to know is, that even though there was a time when they were not your child, there will never-ever again be a time when they are not your child !

The Apostle Paul puts it so well in Romans 8:15 when he writes: *"For you did not receive the spirit of bondage again to fear... but you received the Spirit of adoption by whom we cry out: 'Abba, Father'".* That expression could be translated "Daddy, Dear Daddy"!

Look also at Ephesians 1:5

TRUTH # 8: YOU HAVE BEEN DECLARED RIGHTEOUS — JUSTIFIED

A great theologian of the last century, L.S. Chafer, told his students to think of the term **"justified"** as: **"Just as if I'd never sinned"** !

The following verses reinforce this idea:
Romans 3:24
Romans 5: 1, & 9
1 Corinthians 6:11

TRUTH # 9: YOU WERE DELIVERED FROM SATAN'S KINGDOM

"He has delivered us from the power of darkness and conveyed (transferred) *us into the kingdom of the Son of His love!"* Colossians 1:13

...AND TRANSFERRED INTO GOD'S KINGDOM...

"Having wiped out the handwriting of requirements that was against us which was contrary to us and He has taken it out of the way...having nailed it to the cross. Having disarmed principalities and powers, He made a public spectacle of them, triumphing over them in it." Colossians 2: 14 & 15

See also: John 18:36 & 37

TRUTH # 10: YOU ARE ON A SECURE FOUNDATION...

"For no other foundation can anyone lay than that which is laid." 1 Corinthians 3:11

See: Ephesians 2:20

A GIFT FROM GOD, THE FATHER, TO HIS SON...

"And I give them eternal life and they shall never perish, neither shall anyone snatch them out of My hand... My Father, who has given them

to Me is greater than all and no one is able to snatch them out of My Father's hand.
John 10:28 & 29

See also John 17: 2,6,9,11,12 & 24

TRUTH # 11: YOU CAN NOW BE DELIVERED FROM THE FLESH (old habits)–see #20

"Keep walking in the Spirit and you will find yourself not fulfilling the lusts of the flesh."
Galatians 5:16–(my own translation)

The following verses reinforce this truth:
Romans 7:18
Philippians 3:3
Colossians 2:11

TRUTH # 12: YOU ARE NOW A MEMBER OF GOD'S "FOREVER FAMILY" — HIS CHURCH

"But you are a chosen generation, a royal priesthood, a holy nation, His own special people that you may proclaim the praises of Him who called you out of darkness into His marvellous light... who once were not a people but are now the people of God who had not obtained mercy but now have obtained mercy..."
1 Peter 2:9 & 10

See also: Matthew 16:18 and Titus 2:14

TRUTH # 13: YOU ARE UNDER GOD'S CONSTANT CARE AND ATTENTION !
OBJECTS OF: HIS LOVE

"But God who is rich in mercy, because of His great love with which He loved us, even when we were dead in trespasses, made us alive together with Christ — (for by Grace you have been saved) and raised us up together and made us sit together in heavenly places in Christ Jesus."
Ephesians 2:4-6

John 3:16 & 17
2 Timothy 1:7

HIS PEACE AND STABILITY

"Peace I leave with you, My peace I give unto you. Not as the world give, give I unto you...Let not your heart be troubled, neither let it be afraid."
John 14:27

See also: Romans 5:2
1 Peter 1:5
Philippians 4:6 & 7

HIS SERVICE

"I AM the true vine and My Father is the vinedresser. Every branch in Me that does not bear fruit, He takes away (or lifts up) *and every branch that bears fruit He prunes that it may bear more fruit. You are already clean because of*

the Word which I have spoken. Abide in Me and I in you. As the branch cannot bear fruit unless it abides in the vine neither can you unless you abide in me. I AM the vine and you are the branches. He who abides in Me and I in him bears much fruit, for without Me you can do nothing." John 15: 1-5

What do you think of when you read the word *"abide"*? Jesus uses the idea of a Vine and its branches. How else might you describe the action of abiding?

See also: John 17:18
1 Corinthians 15:58
Ephesians 4:7

HIS INSTRUCTION

"For the Grace of God that brings salvation has appeared to all men, teaching us that denying ungodliness and worldly lusts we should live soberly, righteously and Godly in the present age, looking for the blessed hope and glorious appearing of our great God and Savior Jesus Christ, who gave Himself for us, that He might redeem us from every lawless deed and purify for Himself His own special people zealous for good works..." Titus 2:10-14

Isaiah 50: 4 & 5

HIS POWER

"For God has not given us a spirit of fear, but of power, and of love, and of a sound mind."
2 Timothy 1:7
Ephesians 1:19

HIS FAITHFULNESS

"And Jesus came and spoke to them saying, 'All authority has been given to Me in heaven and on earth. Go, therefore, and make disciples of all nations Baptizing them in the name of the Father, and of the Son, and of the Holy Spirit. Teaching them to observe all things that I have commanded you, and lo, I am with you always even to the end of the age...Amen'"
Matthew 28:18-20

HIS COMFORT

"Now may our Lord Jesus Christ Himself and our God and Father who has loved us and given us everlasting consolation and good hope by Grace, comfort your hearts and establish you in every good word and work..."
2 Thessalonians 2: 16 & 17

HIS PRAYERS

"Who is he who condemns? It is Christ who died, and furthermore is risen, who is even at the right hand of God, who also makes intercession for us..." Romans 8:34

See also: Hebrews 7:25, Hebrews 9:2, 14

TRUTH # 14: YOU ARE A JOINT HEIR WITH CHRIST

"And if children then heirs, heirs of God and joint heirs with Christ. If indeed we suffer with Him that we may also be glorified together."
Romans 8:17

See also: Ephesians 1:14
Colossians 3:24
Hebrews 9:15
1 Peter 1:4

TRUTH # 15: YOU NOW HAVE NEW WORK TO DO

WITNESSES

"But you shall receive power when the Holy Spirit has come upon you, and you shall be witnesses to Me in Jerusalem, and in Judea, and Samaria, and to the end of the earth..."   Acts 1:8

PARTNERS WITH CHRIST

"For we are His workmanship created in Christ Jesus for good works, which God prepared beforehand that we should walk in them."
Ephesians 2:10

See also: Colossians 3:4
1 Corinthians 1:9

MINISTERS OF CHRIST
"Not that we are sufficient of ourselves to think of anything as being from ourselves, but our sufficiency is from God, who also made us sufficient as ministers of the New Covenant not of the letter but of the Spirit, for the letter kills but the Spirit gives life." 2 Corinthians 3:5 & 6
See also: 2 Corinthians 6:4

AMBASSADORS FOR CHRIST
"Now then, we are ambassadors, as though God were pleading through us, we implore you on Christ's behalf, be reconciled to God..."
2 Corinthians 5:20

LIVING LETTERS FROM GOD
"You are our epistle (letter) known and read by all men. Clearly you are our epistle of Christ ministered by us written not with ink but by the Spirit of the living God, not on tablets of stone, but on tablets of flesh... that is of the heart."
2 Corinthians 3: 2& 3

TRUTH # 16: YOU ARE NOW LIGHT AND SALT IN THE WORLD...
"For you were once darkness, but now you are light in the Lord." Ephesians 5:8

See also: Matthew 5:13
1 Thessalonians 5:4

TRUTH # 17: YOU HAVE ALL THAT THE HOLY SPIRIT DOES...

NEW BIRTH
"That which is born of flesh is flesh, and that which is born of the Spirit is Spirit." John 3: 6

SPIRITUAL BAPTISM
"I saw the Spirit descending from heaven like a dove, and He remained on Him. I did not know Him, but He who sent me to Baptize with water said to me, upon whom you see the Spirit descending and remaining on Him, this is He who Baptizes with the Holy Spirit. And I have seen and testified that this is the Son of God."
John 1: 32–34

See also: Acts 1:5
1 Corinthians 12: 13

LIVES IN YOU...
"But this He spoke concerning the Spirit, whom those believing in Him would receive, for the Holy Spirit was not yet given because Jesus was not yet glorified." John 7: 39

See also: Romans 5: 5
1 Corinthians 3:16
1 Corinthians 6:19
Galatians 4:6
1 John 3:24

SEALS YOU INTO GOD'S FAMILY — <u>FOREVER</u>

"Now He who establishes us with you in Christ and has annointed us is God, who also has sealed us and given us the Spirit in our hearts as a guarantee." 2 Corinthians 1: 21 & 22

See also: Ephesians 4:30

GIVES YOU ONE OR MORE SPIRITUAL GIFTS
"But the manifestation of the Spirit is given to each one for the profit of all."
1 Corinthians 12: 7

See also: 1 Corinthians 13: 1 & 2

TRUTH # 18: YOU ARE NOW GLORIFIED !

"Moreover, whom He predestined, these He also called, whom He called, these He also justified, and whom He justified, these He also glorified."
Romans 8: 30

Discuss together what the Apostle Paul was expressing when he used the word *"glorified"*.

TRUTH # 19: YOU ARE NOW COMPLETE IN GOD'S EYES

"And you are complete in Him, who is the Head of all principality and power.." Colossians 2:10

A great way to illustrate this is to use a lense from someone's glasses to represent Christ and explain that God the Father now sees us as *"complete"* or *"righteous"* as He looks at us through the lense of His Son.

Philippians 3:9... *and become one with Him. I no longer count on my own righteousness through obeying the law; rather, I become righteous through faith in Christ. For God's way of making us right with Himself depends on faith.*

TRUTH # 20: YOU CAN NOW *(THROUGH THE POWER OF CHRIST'S DEATH AND RESURRECTION)* ERASE ALL <u>SCAR TISSUE</u> FROM THE PAST...

<u>Scar tissue</u> includes sins, hurts, guilt, shame, past abuse and injury in your soul and brain.

"But He was wounded for our transgressions, He was bruised for our iniquities, and by His stripes we are healed."   Isaiah 53: 5

See also: Psalm 103: 12
               Isaiah 1:18
               Isaiah 43:25
               Isaiah 44:22

(originally compiled by L.S. Chafer and edited by Dick Lowey)

SO HERE YOU ARE!
Let me give you my Paraphrase of a Paraphrase:

[Paraphrase of Eugene Peterson's version of ROMANS 8—by Dick Lowey]

With the arrival of JESUS—the Messiah — the terrible inability to please a HOLY GOD is resolved... Those who CHOOSE HIM enter into the sphere of: "CHRIST—IN-US" —

And they no longer need to live under a continous black cloud.

— —A new power is in operation— —

The Spirit of life in Christ—like a strong wind—has magnificently —CLEARED THE AIR—freeing you from... a frustrated life of ugly victimization at the hands of sin and death!!

God went for the jugular when He sent His own Son...He didn't deal with the problem as something remote—unimportant—[OR IMPOSSIBLE!!!] In His Son – JESUS—He personally took on the human condition—entered the disordered mess of struggling humanity—in order to set it right—once and for all.

The law—weakened [as it always was by human inability] could never have done this!! The law always ended up being used as a "band-aid" on sin... instead of—THE DEEP HEALING OF IT!!

...and – now—what the law-code demanded — ... but couldn't produce]—is accomplished as we go on trusting God...

INSTEAD OF RE-DOUBLING OUR OWN PUNY EFFORTS We are to... simply EMBRACE and COOPERATE WITH .... what the SPIRIT OF GOD is doing in us and through us!!!

THOSE WHO THINK THEY CAN DO IT ON THEIR OWN—end up—OBSESSED—with—measuring their own "moral muscle" BUT—THEY HAVE TO FAKE IT IN REAL LIFE!!!

However—those who trust God's action for them —and now IN & THRU THEM— FIND GOD'S SPIRIT AT WORK !!!—[THE LIVING—-BREATHING —-GOD!!!]

Obsession with SELF—in these matters—is a "dead-end"... ATTENTION TO GOD—CAN LEAD US OUT INTO THE OPEN...—INTO A SPACIOUS,—FREE—LIFE —through any and all circumstances!!!

FOCUSING ON SELF IS THE OPPOSITE OF FOCUSING ON GOD!!!

Anyone completely absorbed in self...IGNORES GOD......and ends up thinking more about self than God.... [or thinking about God only in terms of selfish desires] ... When we do this we ignore who God is... what He wants...and what He is doing... GOD IS NOT PLEASED AT BEING IGNORED!!!

But if God—HIMSELF—has—TAKEN UP RESIDENCE—in your life. It is totally inappropriate to be thinking more of yourself than of Him!!!

[Anyone—of course—-who has not invited this –invisible— but clearly present God [the Spirit of Christ]—into their lives... won't know what we're taking about...]

But for you – who welcome Him—[in whom He dwells –even though you still experience the limitations of sin—] you, yourself,—EXPERIENCE LIFE ON GOD'S TERMS...!!!. Therefore —it stands to reason—doesn't it?—that—

If the ALIVE and PRESENT GOD [who raised Jesus from the dead] MOVES INTO YOUR LIFE, He'll do the same thing in you that He did in Jesus— "MAKING YOU ALIVE — TO HIMSELF !!!? WITH HIS SPIRIT LIVING IN YOU—YOUR BODY HAS THE POTENTIAL OF BEING AS ALIVE AS JESUS!!!

[So you see we don't owe that—old—"do it yourself" life—one fleeting thought!!!] There's nothing in it for us...nothing at all!!!

The best thing to do is GIVE IT A DECENT BURIAL... AND GET ON WITH YOUR NEW LIFE... THERE ARE THINGS TO DO....AND PLACES TO GO!!!

This resurrection life [you received from God] Is NOT A TIMID – "GRAVE TENDING" LIFE...IT IS WILDLY EXPECTANT!!

Greeting God with:... "What's next, DADDY?"... God's Spirit continually speaks to our hearts... CONFIRMING WHO WE REALLY ARE!!!

We know Him as Father—-for we know ourselves as His children!!!

And we know we are going to get what's coming to us [though, we don't deserve it] — AN

UNBELIEVEABLE INHERITANCE!!! —As we go through whatever Christ sends our way...

If we go through hard times with Him, then aren't we ,certainly, going to go through good times with Him?

That's why I don't think there's any comparison between...

The present hard times...

And...the coming good times...

The created world, itself, can hardly wait for what's coming next!!!

All of creation is being more or less held back... God reins it in until all is ready—READY TO BE RELEASED AT THE SAME MOMENT—INTO GLORIOUS TIMES AHEAD !!!

MEANWHILE—

THE JOY OF ANTICIPATION INCREASES!!!

All around us we see a "pregnant" creation... The difficult times of pain throughout the world are simply birth pangs!!!

It's not only around us ....it's within us!!

We're feeling...

............"BIRTH PANGS!!!"

These weak and broken down bodies of ours are yearning for full deliverance... and transformation...

BUT HEY.............

That's why waiting needn't drag us down anymore...

Anymore than it discourages a pregnant mother-to-be...

Indeed—-we are made more mature in the waiting...

We, of course, don't see what's happening...

But the longer we wait, the "bigger" we become...

And the greater will be our joy in the realization of our hope.

MEANWHILE...
IF WE DON'T KNOW HOW TO PRAY....
IT DOESN'T REALLY MATTER...
HE DOES OUR PRAYING FOR US!!!........AND "IN US"!!!
MAKING PRAYERS OUT OF OUR SIGHS AND GROANING!!!
HE KNOWS US BETTER THAN WE KNOW OURSELVES !
THEREFORE.....—HE KEEPS US IN TOUCH WITH HIMSELF!!!

This is why we can really believe...

Because we love Him....

Every event in our lives is worked into something good!!!

God knew, from the beginning, what He was doing...

He decided, from the start, to shape the lives of those who would

choose Him, into the pattern of His Son!!!

The Son stands first in line of THE NEW HUMANITY!!! —RESTORED!!!

We see the "God-intended" shape of our lives there in Him!!!

At just the right time—- God called each of His children into His family—BY NAME—

Set them on a secure foundation...[Himself]

And now—He stays with them...to the end...

Gloriously completing the work He began!!!

SO—WHAT DO YOU THINK?

With God on our side like this— HOW CAN WE LOSE??

If God put everything on the line for us...

Embracing our human condition and...

Exposing Himself to the worst...

Sending His Son for us...GIVING US HIS BEST...

Is there anything less He won't do for us???

AND...

WHO WOULD DARE TANGLE WITH GOD BY CONDEMNING GOD'S CHOSEN???? WHO WOULD EVEN DARE POINT A FINGER? THE ONE WHO HAS THE RIGHT TO ACCUSE US—

DIED FOR US...WAS RAISED TO LIFE FOR US... AND—-IS...THIS VERY MOMENT —-.. STICKING UP FOR US !.....

CAN ANYONE DRIVE A WEDGE BETWEEN US AND GOD'S LOVE FOR US??

NO WAY!!!

NOT TROUBLE...

NOT HARD TIMES...
NOT OTHER PEOPLE'S CRITICISM...
NOT ECONOMIC LACK...
NOT HOMELESSNESS...
NOT OTHER THREATENING CIRCUMSTANCES.....
NOT PEOPLE'S GOSSIP...
NOT EVEN THE WORST ACTS FROM OTHERS...
THE WORST THAT THEY CAN DO TO US IS KILL US!!!
WE CAN EVEN FACE THIS!!! BECAUSE OF JESUS!

LISTEN....
I AM ABSOLUTELY CONVINCED THAT —NOTHING...
LIVING OR DEAD...ANGELIC OR DEMONIC...
WHAT HAPPENS...TODAY OR TOMORROW....
WHAT'S HIGH OR WHAT'S LOW...
THINKABLE OR UNTHINKABLE...

ABSOLUTELY NOTHING ...
CAN GET BETWEEN US AND GOD'S LOVE...
THIS LOVE JUST CAN'T BE REMOVED!!!
BECAUSE—JESUS ———OUR SOVEREIGN LORD———
HAS DEFENDED US!!!!!
[SO, THERE!]

Chapter 3

THE TWO LEVEL STRUCTURE OF SALVATION

UPPER LEVEL = ETERNAL DESTINY
Our Position
(due to His redemptive work on the cross)
Only Changes Once!
(see Hebrews 10: 13-14 et al.)

The Unbeliever

> **In Adam (Eve)**
> We Are LOST
> Headed For HELL
> 2 Thess. 1:8- 9, I Jn. 5:11-13
> (The absence of God)
> The fruit of the fall of Adam & Eve
> CUT OFF FROM GOD

The Believer

> **In Christ**
> We Are FOUND (SAVED)
> (1st John 5:11-13)
> Headed For
> HEAVEN=United with God
> TOTALLY A GIFT, PERMANENT, UNCHANGEABLE!
> (Romans 8:1)

<<THIS TAKES PLACE ONCE   IN THE HEAVENLIES (Eph. 2:6)>>

Timeline: **(PAST)** >>>>>>>>>>>>>>>>>>>>>+ +>>>>>>>>>>>>>> **(PRESENT & FUTURE)**

P O I N T | O F F A I T H

LOWER LEVEL = OUR EXPERIENCE
(This Represents Our Experience on the Earth)

Walk in Adam

> **THE SELF DIRECTED LIFE**
> Self-Will Driven
> Self-Centered
> Selfish
> (I need, I want, I must have)

Walk in Christ

> **THE SPIRIT LIFE**
> Chooses God's Will First
> Self is Centered in God
> Focuses on God and Others

(When we walk in the flesh, we lose our freedom, but NOT our Salvation. Confession restores our Walk in Christ)

THE UPPER LEVEL

In time, before you met Jesus, your heavenly destiny was without any personal contact with God. You were choosing, whether you knew it or not, to head away from God and therefore towards Hell (the state of being separated from God.) This was the fruit (the result) of the fall from God by Adam and Eve when they chose to look to themselves to gain the knowledge of the tree of Good and Evil. This is called 'Original Sin'. As a result of their actions, Adam and Eve had to leave the Garden (God's realm) to experience what life was like living by their own wisdom. Thus we (the human race) live in and through 'Adam'. We have a disease that we cannot heal or cure which we inherited from 'Adam'. Only God, through Jesus Christ's saving work, can, as Oswald Chambers wrote in 'My Utmost for His Highest', "Jesus did not come to save us from our 'sins'. He came to save us from our 'Sin Disease' (Self-Will Directed Life)."

Thus God planned before creation began to save as many humans as possible, based on their personal choice for Him. God is a personal and relational God. He 'wants to be wanted' and He created us to be able to live with Him on a personal relational basis. Here's my way of explaining it using Romans 8:29: God in His foreknowledge knew, if given the right conditions and circumstances, that you would choose Him. Based on this, He chose to provide those conditions. Thus He chose you before you chose Him! He chose, ahead of time, to change your eternal destiny. When the right moment arrived, you were given the ability (as a result of Christ's finished work) to choose Him.

And you did! Glory be to God!! From that moment on, you were a new creation in Christ. A new you, ready and able to live a new life of 'contact' (in relationship) with God. This heavenly transfer of eternal destiny takes place **'only once, is permanent, and unchangeable i.e.: (irreversible)!'** You have now become His **forever!** (See the previous chapter on 'The 20 Truths')

THE GOSPEL GATE
'A Helpful Illustration'

I find this a helpful illustration from a biblical viewpoint. 'The Gospel Gate of Christ's Salvation' has a message on both sides of the gate. On the front side, as you walk through the gate, it reads, **'Come Through This Gate All Who Choose Christ'.** What is written on the reverse side of the Gate, which can only be seen by looking back, is, **'I Chose You To Come Through This Gate'** signed, God. This message is the first one in the Upper Level. The message seen as you look back is written to and for believers only! It is not for the 'world' lest they would interpret it as meaning that God has chosen some to become believers and others to remain unbelievers. **Be at ease!**

REMEMBER GOD'S CHOICE IS BASED ON YOUR CHOICE. Yet... it appears that these two principles of **'Free Will'** & **'Predestination'** seem to contradict one another. Meaning: If you choose one then you must reject the other and vice versa. This is only true if you try to understand them as two separate principles. Before concluding this, consider the Jewish principle of **'Paradox'**.

As told by my dear Jewish friend, Paul Kaufman, "What does a 'paradox' mean? It means 'a pair of 'Docs' conversing [ch, ch, boom (symbols followed by a short drum roll)]. Gotcha didn't I? Come on you can admit it. Oh well, back to the dilemma at hand. An example of paradox can be found in Philippians 2:12-13 which reads as follows:

12 Therefore, my beloved, as you have always obeyed, not as in My presence only, but now much more in My absence, work out your own salvation with fear and trembling;

13 for it is God who works in you both to will and to do for His good pleasure.

If you understand these directives as standing alone, you are trapped in the dilemma that by choosing one, you automatically exclude the other and vice versa. Therefore if you focus on 'work out your salvation' then you are right back into works; what one does, as the means to gain 'salvation' (God's acceptance). Thus, 'Grace' is lost or rendered useless."

"If you focus on, 'it is God who works within you', then you end up passively waiting for God to 'do it' to and in you without your having to participate in the process, and we are led to conclude that any effort on our part is ineffective or totally useless. Practically

The Two Level Structure of Salvation

speaking, you end up with both principles proving to be useless. However, there is a way to reconcile these two irreconcilable truths."

As Paul Kaufman goes on to say, "A Paradox is the way to connect two seemingly exclusive concepts together. To make this possible, Paradox has you hold these two truths in tension like a 'high wire'. If the wire is taut, one is able to walk between the two points. In this case, *"Work Out Your Salvation"* is connected by the word **'for'** (or this word could be translated **'because'** in place of **'for'**). Now it reads like this paraphrase, *'Work out your salvation....... because God is already* (due to your choosing to trust in Jesus) *working in you both to will and do according to His good pleasure.'*"

This is how a Paradox works. Scripture teaches we are completely unable to both will and work out our salvation through our own power. Therefore without God's saving Grace and the continuing inflow of His Grace, by means of the Holy Spirit, we fail. Yet as we believe and continue to believe, through the daily surrender of our will to God, we experience in our activities, (worshiping, praying and fellowship with other followers of Christ) a progressive increase in awareness of the Lord's presence. He challenges, encourages, and sometimes provokes us, into learning and practicing our new life in Christ as we walk towards 'spiritual maturity'."

This maturity (gaining and acting in wisdom) like our physical growth from childhood to adulthood, is not a straight line; growing from success to success. Rather we are more like a child with equal parts of wonder, and delight, trying out new things as well as defiant, selfish, wanting what we want with no thought or concern for anyone else. We grew and continue to grow through trial and error, through correction and consequences. So do we in living a life under the guidance of Jesus through the Holy Spirit. The essential concept to grasp in the paradox of Phil. 2:12-13 as well as in the paradox of **'free will' and 'predestination'** is that we can never fully grasp how God works in and through us. It is a mystery. That He does this work in and through us there is no doubt, but all we can finally say about the process is it remains a mystery. What results from this realization is that we have been, and will continue throughout our lives to be 'transformed' into the likeness of Jesus.'

Make no mistake; this living in time (the Lower Level on the chart) is not an easy process. It has been likened to iron ore that is put into the furnace where the temperature is turned up so high that it melts. The impurities then rise to the surface to be skimmed off, resulting in only the pure metal remaining. That does not sound like fun. And it isn't. Be not afraid for God will take you through this process in order to equip you to glorify Him and be of use to others. Even the worst elements of your lifestyle God takes and turns into Christ's likeness. What we are most in need of is a 'character transplant'. We need God to take our 'character' (the heredity of sin) out and

The Two Level Structure of Salvation

transplant His 'character' into us. This is slowly happening, but we usually aren't aware of it until others tell us that we have become, 'somehow different in the way we respond to people & life.' Occasionally, we will recognize this transforming process in ourselves; though always in hindsight and with equal doses of astonishment, wonder and childlike joy.

So is it with '**The Gospel Gate**'. We cannot rationally see how the two work together. Only that they do! But the beautiful result can be a new freedom in our lives with Jesus.

Martin Luther said, "Sin boldly that Grace may abound." I take this to mean that we are called to live, but not to live in fear of making mistakes, or making a mess of things hurting ourselves and others, etc. Realize that we have done this and will continue to do this. God has provided for our failures through natural consequences, confession, restitution, and serving others. He is the God of more than second chances.

'**Predestination**' is one of God's safety nets for when we mess up. In other words, what I've come to believe is that God says, "Relax, live freely and boldly in and through Me because, in the end, I've got you covered."

I do not mean this statement to be a license for us to do whatever we want, but rather to have our wants changed by God. The point is that Christians have and can become so afraid of making missteps or mistakes that they have a tendency to 'play it safe' or to conform to what others say is right for them to do.

However, the Kingdom of God has never been advanced in a safe nice, timid, way. Rather, the Kingdom has been advanced by those willing to step outside of their comfort zone and take some risks, (go on an adventure). Just check out any character in the Old Testament Scriptures: Noah, Abraham, Sarah, Jacob, Moses, Rahab, Gideon, Samson, Ruth, Esther, David, the prophets, Nehemiah, Isaiah, and Jonah. Investigate Mary and Joseph, John the Baptist, Mary Magdalene, Mary (of Mary and Martha), Lazarus, the disciples, the Apostle Paul, Barnabas, Silas, Mark, and Timothy in the New Testament. Read the life stories of any of these 'saints' listed here. You'll learn that their lives were messy, not pure and clean. That's right, messy. What a bunch of ragamuffins, no names, losers, liars, deceivers, timid, full of fear, self-righteous, pompous, and full of ego. In other words, they were just like you and me. (What a relief!) And God worked in and through their lives.

Oh, by the way, don't worry or be afraid that you are unequipped to advance the Kingdom in the unique ways God has for you. Relax already! 'God does not call the equipped. He equips the called'. Or ' God doesn't use the able. He uses the available.

<u>THE LOWER LEVEL</u>

There is also **The Lower Level**. This is the level at which we live out our daily lives on the earth. It is often referred to as our "Walk with Christ", which started when we began an active relationship with Jesus.

For example, take a look at the conversation between Jesus and Peter when Jesus washed the disciples feet (John 13: 10ff). Peter wanted Jesus to wash his whole body. Jesus replied by telling Peter, *"He that is bathed (all over), only needs to wash his feet....."* (feet are made for walking). Jesus is referring to the experiential need to confess our sins because it is only through confessing that we can release the hold that our negative behavior has over us. When we have emptied out our sins to God in private and/or to someone who will listen to us without judgment, as well as keep what we share completely confidential, then the forgiveness that Jesus pronounced on the cross can begin to become real for us.

A metaphor, though earthy, is when you have to throw up, you cannot eat (nor do you have any desire to do so) until you finally surrender and throw up (throw it out of you). There is then, space inside you to eat again, though it may take some time to feel the desire to eat. Confession keeps you honest and real with the Lord (which is one of His deepest desires for you) as well as keeps you real and honest with yourself and others. Remember, He already knows what you are thinking and feeling. The problem is within us. We are the ones who are afraid to be real. You, like all of us, will probably never be 'absolutely' real with Jesus. We can strive to be rigorously honest.

And practicing these principles causes a deeper awareness of Christ.

If you look at the chart on the first page of this chapter, you'll notice in the lower right hand corner there is a 'hole' in the bottom of the box labeled 'The Spirit Life'. I'm trying to illustrate here that this is the only level where you can "fall out" by walking away from Christ. Please note that allowing 'unconfessed sin' to remain in your life, in no way causes you to lose your salvation (**The Upper Level**). It only takes away your freedom in Him (**Lower Level**).

Take a look at the life of David as reflected in I Kings, Psalm 32, and Psalm 51. When you 'grieve' or 'quench' the Holy Spirit, you progressively lose the desire to relate with God. Eventually, if you continue to walk away, you become hardened toward God through lack of confession. Then God becomes like the hound in the famous poem by Francis Thompson, 'The Hound of Heaven'. In the poem, the writer speaks of being chased, pursued by the hound whom he knows is God. Wherever he goes, there is the hound coming up behind him. Eventually, it becomes clear that there is no place to hide. He then stops running and surrenders to God (the hound).

In recovery circles, this 'coming to the end of yourself' is called 'hitting bottom', or 'Point Zero'. It is such a relief to stop running and allow God to have His way with you based on your once again turning your 'will and life over to Him', confessing your sins, making amends to those you have hurt, including

God and yourself even though it may not be easy or without fear to do so. In the process of doing these things, you will begin to feel freer and lighter. If you are willing to follow this path, you will experience — in time — God's forgiveness and restoration becoming a reality within you. It takes time, but it will happen.

Note: Unconfessed sin can eventually lead to physical death.

The Law of Liberty

The phrase "The Law of Liberty" can be found in James 1:25 and James 2:12 and means 'The Law of Freedom' or 'The Law of Love'. Taken along with Paul's statement in Romans 13:10, it is the believer's way of fulfilling 'The Law' in his or her life. Let's unpack this idea. 'Liberty' or 'Freedom', in everyday terms, means 'doing what you want to do'. But what if the thing you want to do is morally wrong? Paul wrestles with this problem in Romans 7:14-25. (I'll discuss this passage later in the chapter.)

Mae West, a movie star from the '30's, once said, "Why is it that everything that I want to do is illegal, immoral, or fattening?" As Christians, we often feel the same way. This dilemma is resolved when we connect what the Apostle Paul wrote in Romans 8:1 with 1st Corinthians 6:12 & 10:23. (Romans 8:1: *"There is therefore now no condemnation to those who are in Christ Jesus."* 1st Corinthians 6:12 & 10:23.... Paul says that now everything is lawful (permissible) for the believer. This means that Christians will not be held guilty for any wrong deed, past, present or future, because Jesus Christ paid the full price for every sin a believer has committed or ever will commit. Therefore, everything is permissible!

But, Paul's verses do not stop at the first statement. They go on to say, <u>and this is crucial</u>, that everything isn't constructive (to our and other people's advantage). Therefore the basis for good behavior changes from '*should* do' to '*want* to do'.

Let me break it down this way. Freedom is usually defined as 'Doing what you want to do.' But what if the thing you want to do brings misery? If you are in Christ, the answer would rather obviously be that you wouldn't want to do it. If what you desire is constructive, it would stand to reason that you would **want** to do it. If these two statements are true for you as a Christian, then **You Are Truly Free**.

Take note: Freedom, for the Christian, consists of wanting or desiring to do good or what is right. As a Christian, your motivation to do good is no longer based on '**<u>having</u> to do right in order to gain God's approval**'. Rather, your motivation to do good is based on your '**<u>desire</u> to do good**' which, in turn, rises from your response to Jesus's unconditional love for you. Your desire to please Christ arises out of your '**thanks-living**', the desire, born from a thankful heart, to give to the Lord.

When you love someone, the desire arises to give sacrificially to that person out of your love for

The Two Level Structure of Salvation

them. However, when you struggle with desiring to give to the other, you can turn to Jesus and ask Him to change your desire (your heart). God loves these kinds of prayers. An example would be that of the father of the epileptic/demon possessed son who when Jesus asked him if he believed He could heal the son, replied, *"I believe, help my unbelief."* Another way of putting this request is, "I want to be willing. Change my unwillingness."

In the midst of this talk of how you, in Christ, pray for the desire to do good, comes a harsh reality. It is this: Our 'old sin nature', in the Lower Level, is still with us. Therefore, it is crucial to properly understand what God means by 'Sin'. The problem for many people in the general public, particularly in the 'West' is an incomplete understanding of what 'sin' is. Many people (Christians and non-Christians alike) assume that sin is simply the 'bad' things that we do or think. Therefore they do not understand how they can be under God's judgment when they haven't done anything 'bad' or 'really bad'. They say, 'But I'm a good person.' By this logic, they aren't 'sinners' because 'sinners' do 'bad' things. This thinking makes logical sense and leads to a logical conclusion. But their conclusion is false because they hold an incomplete understanding of sin.

God's understanding of 'Sin' is something quite different and more foundational than 'sin is doing bad things'. Oswald Chambers, in his classic devotional

'My Utmost for His Highest', accurately sums up what God means by 'Sin' when he writes,

"The nature of sin is not immorality and wrong doing, but the nature of self-realization which leads us to say, 'I am my own god.' This nature may exhibit itself in proper morality or in improper morality, but it always has a common basis—my claim to my right to myself. When our Lord faced either people, with all the forces of evil in them, or people who were clean-living, moral, and upright, He paid no attention to the moral degradation of one group, or the moral attainment of the other group. He looked at something that we do not see, namely the nature of man (see John 2:25).

Sin is something that I am born with and cannot touch—only God touches sin through redemption. It is through the cross of Christ that God redeemed the whole human race from the possibility of damnation through the heredity of sin. God nowhere holds a person responsible for having the heredity of sin, and does not condemn anyone because of it. Condemnation comes when I realize that Jesus Christ came to deliver me from the heredity of sin, and yet, I refuse to let Him do so" (October 5).

'Sin' therefore is not what we do or don't do. I heard Peter Gilquist (of Campus Crusade) in the 1960's describe sin in a way that I have never forgotten. He calls 'SIN'

'SIM'. It means **S**elf **I**nduced **M**isery. (It has also been called: 'SIN': **S**elfish **I**n **N**ature.)

The Two Level Structure of Salvation

There are two sides to 'the 'flesh', the 'strong, defiant' side and the 'indulgent' side. The 'strong' side produces 'fallen goodness' or a self-generated goodness that defies God, consciously or unconsciously, by saying and seemingly demonstrating that they do not need God in order to be good. Another way to describe the strong side of the flesh is to say that it is characterized by 'righteousness on display'.

The 'indulgent' side of the flesh typically produces 'common immorality' that seems to be, on the surface, both shameless and guiltless. (That which one generation calls immoral can and often does become the accepted morality of the next generation.)

I find that looking at 'Sin' this way makes it easier to turn from it, especially when I look at it in terms of being selfish, self-centered, or self-will driven. You can rationalize or explain any particular behavior, thought, or attitude, but when you see it as based in self (which Christians, particularly in our new nature in Christ, dislike) two things are likely to occur. First, you are more likely to take responsibility for your actions when you see them as rooted in self. Secondly, you are more likely to be moved to turn these thoughts and behaviors over to the Lord to deal with.

Doing this opens the desire to pursue that which is, "good, pure, etc....(see Phil. 4). That is, you desire to do what is constructive for yourself and others. Growing towards maturity in Christ means that, *"you keep walking, with intention, by the Spirit and you will find yourself not fulfilling the works of the flesh"* (Galatians 5:16- my own translation). This freedom does away with guilt and misery because, after all, we are only doing what we want. The difference is that you, with the Holy Spirit, continually discover that what you want changes.

Yet the truth you will discover in life, is that you stumble, mess up, hurt yourself and others, even if you don't intend to, as you move towards maturity in Christ. As perfect yet imperfect Christians, we often forget that we are not journeying alone. Jesus is walking alongside and in us, encouraging, affirming, challenging, even provoking us towards being transformed into His Likeness.

We are also not alone because the Christian walk is to be done in community. Here is good news for us when we stumble. Jesus has provided for us a 'safety net'. This is the purpose of confession, both to God and our fellow-Christians. *"If we confess our sins, God is just and right to forgive us and cleanse us from all unrighteousness."* (1st John 1:9). Once again, He has us covered. He has thought of everything. Your goal, on a human level, is 'progress' not 'perfection'. So relax. Besides, when we are instructed in the scriptures to 'be perfect', the word perfect does not mean what we normally think it does. In the Greek, perfect slants more toward meaning, to be 'whole' or 'mature'. Although, in the Upper Level, Christ has already made us perfect, positionally in Him. We have the 'righteousness of Christ in us' (2nd Corinthians 5:21).

The Two Level Structure of Salvation

Dave Ramsey, the Christian financial counselor puts it this way, "How do you learn to make good choices (act in and with Wisdom)? From experience! How do you gain experience? From making bad choices." To unpack the struggle between what you self-centeredly desire and what God desires for you to desire, we will now look to Paul's own struggle with this war within.

Paul eloquently describes this 'war within' as an ongoing internal struggle in Romans 7: 14-25:

"For we know that the law is spiritual, but I am carnal, sold under sin. For what I am doing, I do not understand. For what I will to do, that I do not practice; but what I hate, that I do. If, then, I do what I will not to do, I agree with the law that it is good. But now, it is no longer I who do it, but sin that dwells in me. For I know that in me (that is, in my flesh) nothing good dwells; for to will is present with me, but how to perform what is good I do not find. For the good that I will to do, I do not do; but the evil I will not to do, that I practice. Now if I do what I will not to do, it is no longer I who do it, but sin that dwells in me. I find then a law, that evil is present with me, the one who wills to do good. For I delight in the law of God according to the inward man. But I see another law in my members, warring against the law of my mind, and bringing me into captivity to the law of sin which is in my members. O wretched man that I am! Who will deliver me from this body of death? I thank God—through Jesus Christ

our Lord! So then, with the mind I myself serve the law of God, but with the flesh the law of sin."

Two principles that you might consider as you look at this passage are: 1) Even though many have attempted to name what the behavior was that Paul struggled with, Paul does not mention the content of his struggle. He knew that if he did, the focus would be on the content rather than the principle or pattern he wants you to grasp.

2) Paul wrote this passage later in his life with Christ. By then (65 A.D.) he was mature in his walk with Christ. Paul indicates that you will continually have to struggle with this 'war within' throughout your life, as all of us do. Therefore, you (we) must learn how to deal with this struggle.

Thus, as you look to Paul's other 'End of his life teachings', Paul balances out the Romans 7:14-25 passage on his sinful flesh, with scriptures of such encouragement, relief, joy, like a call to battle. Some of those passages are: Romans 8:1-4, Romans 8:18-24, Romans 8:25-39, Philippians 1:6-11, Philippians 4: 11-13 to name a few.

I challenge you to look up these passages and let these truths from the Word of God work their way into your experience because they too add to the 'Safety Net' that God has provided for us as we walk with Jesus Christ.

Chapter 4

"HIS STORY" AND "MY STORY"

REHEARSALS OF THE COMING MESSIAH IN THE OLD AND NEW TESTAMENTS

First of all, I'd like you to consider what I call **"The Centerpiece of the Bible":** Job 19: 23-27

Here is Job — at the height of his suffering. He has lost his family, his wealth, his health. (He has boils all over his body.) He's also rejected by his wife. She tells him to "curse God and die". If that's not bad enough, his friends accuse him of sins, which in their eyes, must be the reason for his trouble.

At this point, God breaks into Job's brain with an Epiphany — a supernatural understanding of His plan for the future.

Job cries out: *"Oh that my words were recorded, that they were written on a scroll, that they were inscribed with an iron tool on lead, or engraved in rock forever. 'I know that my redeemer lives! And in the end, He will stand upon the earth... And after my skin has been destroyed, yet in my flesh, I will see God. I myself will see Him with my own eyes. I and not another... How my heart yearns within me.!!"*

NOTES:

The word for *"redeemer"* means "one who pays the full price for something".

"In the end" means "in a future time."

"After my skin has been destroyed." means "after my death".

The 2nd layer meaning for the phrase, "in my flesh" can also be translated, "in flesh like mine."

The 20th Century Archaeologist and leading Biblical scholar, W. F. Albright put the origin of the writing of Job at 10,000 to 15,000 years BC !! So this is probably the oldest book you can hold in your hands!

REHEARSALS:
1. The Prophecy after Adam and Eve rebelled: Genesis 3:1-13

My Story — His Story

"So the Lord God said to the serpent, because you have done this, cursed are you above all the livestock and all the wild animals. You will crawl on your belly and you will eat dust all the days of your life, and I will put enmity (hostility) between you and the woman — and between your seed (offspring) and hers. He will crush your head, but you shall strike (wound) his heel (appendages).

To the women He said, 'I will greatly increase your pains in childbearing. With pain you will give birth to children... Your desire will be for your husband and he will rule over you...'"

NOTES:

"The seed of the woman" (as opposed to the seed of a man! =Virgin Birth)

"will crush the head" — will render inoperative — the intentions and actions of *"the seed of the serpent".*

2. **Cain and Abel — My Story: Genesis 4:1-10**
   (The requirement of a blood sacrifice is planted in the corporate mindset of God's people. i.e. A blood sacrifice is required for acceptance with God.)
   In the fourth chapter of Genesis we are told about the first murder — we are our brother's keeper!

3. **Noah rescued from the Flood — My Story: Genesis 6: 7 & 8**
   The Ark represents salvation in the midst of a world drowning in sin and lostness.
   Noah means "new man" and also means "rest".

4. **Abraham offers Isaac — His Story: Genesis 22:1-14**
   Question: Why would God require "a father" to offer "his son" as a sacrifice? Is God perhaps providing a "picture" of what He did for us — out of His infinite love? At the last moment, Abraham was told "Don't" + Resurrection.

This story took place on the same mountain less than a mile from Calvary when He Himself did provide The Lamb.

5. **Jacob and Esau — My Story: Genesis 27**
   The name Jacob means "deceiver". But after an encounter with the "God/man" his name is changed to "Israel" which means "chosen". So like us he went from deceiver to chosen.

6. **Jacob wrestles God — My Story: Genesis 32:24-30**
   The wrestling opponent is a "theophany": God in human form.

7. **Joseph is "killed" (sold) — His Story: Genesis 38:18-36**
   Joseph's brothers commit the crime. Joseph is "resurrected" and offers Grace and Forgiveness to his brothers. (Genesis 50:15-21)

8. **Passover in Egypt — His Story: Exodus 12: 1-13**
   When God sees the blood of a lamb, it keeps death away.
   NOTE: The lamb's blood is specifically to be smeared "vertically" and "horizontally" = The Cross?

9. **The Exodus — My Story and His Story: Exodus 15:13–31**
   As you read this passage notice the parallels: Exodus represents conversion from slavery to freedom and headed for a "promised land".

"His Story" And "My Story"

People of God in the wilderness represent the Christian's life in this world, headed for a "promised land" — heaven.

10. Water out of a Rock–The water comes when the rock is struck —
His Story: Exodus 17: 1-7
The Rock represents Jesus
The Water represents Salvation–which came when He was "hit".

11. The Serpent lifted up in the Wilderness
Jesus identifies Himself with this event directly in John 3:14 & 15:
"And as Moses lifted up the Serpent in the wilderness, even so must the Son of Man be lifted up that whoever believes in Him should not perish but have everlasting life."

NOTE: The Bronze Serpent had no poison in it just as Jesus had no sin in Him, yet for a look (faith) this healed the people of their "snake bite" — and by faith we are healed of that ancient "snake bite" from the Garden of Eden!

The Old Testament provides "Pictures" of the redemptive suffering of our Messiah Jesus, in Psalm 22 and Isaiah 53.

The last two verses in the Old Testament speak of John the Baptist announcing the arrival of Jesus:
"Behold I will send you Elijah, the prophet — [John's hero figure) *before the great and dreadful day of the Lord* (the yet to come "tribulation") *.. and He will*

turn the hearts of the fathers to the children and the hearts of the children to their fathers lest I come and strike the earth with a curse.."

Throughout the Old Testament you can find rehearsal after rehearsal after rehearsal of Christ's coming. And then, at the appointed time, Jesus slips into human history.

In fact, Jesus Himself conducts the last "rehearsal" with His disciples — at the Last Supper when He transforms the Passover Feast. It is now a picture of what our Lord fulfilled the very next day when He became the Final Sacrifice–The One True Lamb who takes away the sins of the world.

THE PERFORMANCE: JESUS' DEATH AND RESURRECTION

At the point when it was all finished, I can hear the voice of The Father saying: **"Now I am free to love them! My justice is satisfied. My hatred against that which corrupts and destroys human life has been poured out. All sin is paid for! It is finished !! I have done it! I have set myself free to love them! I can now accept completely anyone who asks for it !"**

QUESTION:
Have you accepted God's total acceptance of you?
He wants ALL of you — He paid the COMPLETE price.

CONCLUSION:

When you do this — make your choice:

Simply...

Believe and Receive —- His acceptance of you.

When this happens, a very exciting thing takes place:

The Two Stories: His Story and Your Story becomes ONE STORY.

You find yourself living a piece of His Story, and as you walk with Him, He gives you the desire and the ability to live for Him! See: Philippians 3.

Chapter 5

TWO FOUNDATIONAL VERSES

Romans 10:17: "Faith comes from hearing and hearing from the Word of God." Romans 10:17

Repeat this verse OUT LOUD. The "heard Word" produces Faith.

Hebrews 11:6: "But without Faith it is impossible to please God, for he who comes to God must believe that He is (present) and He is a rewarder of them that diligently seek Him." Hebrews 11:6

Repeat this verse OUT LOUD.

It is FAITH not works which please God.

So what we need to please God comes from the continual impact of His Word. Throughout the Bible we find that God is not impressed with human effort. But when we come to the New Testament — the Gospel of Grace tells us — not of works — lest any man boast. Ephesians 2: 8&9 says, *"For by Grace are you saved through Faith and that not of yourselves, it is the gift of God."*

The Apostle Paul also states in Romans 10:3 & 4: *"For they* (the Jews) *being ignorant of God's righteousness and seeking to establish their own righteousness, have not submitted to the righteousness of God."*

And in Romans 11:6: *"And if by Grace then it is no longer of works — otherwise Grace is no longer Grace. But if it is of works, it is no longer Grace, otherwise work is no longer work."* What Paul is explaining here is the two are mutually excluside. If you have one, you don't have the other.

Donald Gray Barnhouse states, "Our good works betray us." We cannot shout down the corridors of history to Jesus when He was suffering on the cross and say: **"Not enough Jesus! What You did was not enough!"**

Something to discuss:

Does this mean we are not to DO *anything*?

James tells us in James 2:20: **"*Can't you see that faith without good deeds is useless?*"** He continues in verse 26: **"*Just as the body is dead without breath, so also faith is dead without good works.*"**

Chapter 6

THE THREE LEGGED STOOL

Keeping a balance of these three vital areas of your new life in Christ has proven to be helpful:
1) Word of God (Bible Study on your own and with others)
2) Prayer (alone and with others)
3) Fellowship (Worship and Sharing Christ)

Like a three legged stool, if one or more of these "legs" is neglected by the believer, the life — experience suffers. (We're not as free, happy and full of life as we could be.)

BUT...

This does NOT mean we lose our Salvation. It's just an inappropriate response to our loving Lord. How can we say we love the Lord and then neglect to spend any time with Him?

ASK YOURSELF:
- Are any of these areas of your life "out of balance" or missing?
- Are there other activities or areas of interest in your life that are crowding out one or more of these three vital areas?
- What choices or changes do you need to make (with the help of The Holy Spirit) in order to bring your life into balance?

Chapter 7

"QUIET TIME"

TIME ALONE WITH GOD EVERY DAY– (DEVOTIONS)
Here's a suggested outline that has been effective for many people:

Open with Prayer — telling the Lord the following:

> This day I want You!
> Please give me a teachable, humble spirit
> I want You to change me — take me to the next level so I can praise and glorify You more.
> I admit and confess the following:
> I also accept Your forgiveness and cleansing for:
> Now dear Lord, Lead me to the Scriptures You want me to absorb in Your presence. I desire that You speak to me. I delight in Your presence.
> This day I want to love You and serve You. Please show me how.

"Quiet Time"

Also, would you help the following people who are hurting:

And give faith to those who need Your salvation, Lord:

I willingly pray for those I find difficult to love:

And lastly I ask You, dear Savior, to solve the following problems for me, or help me endure what You are allowing me to go through.

Help me to trust You more fully as we face challenges in my life together.

Lord, I love You.

In Jesus' Name — AMEN

FOR YOUR ON-GOING DEVOTIONAL LIFE:
Books of Daily Devotions I recommend you use are:
"Jesus Calling"–by Sarah Young
"100 Days"–by Joseph Prince
"My Utmost for His Highest"–by Oswald Chambers
"Through the Bible–Through the Year"–by John Stott
"Grace Notes–Daily Readings with a Fellow Pilgrim"–by Philip Yancey
"Experiencing God Day-by-Day" by Henry T. Blackaby & Richard Blackaby

PRACTICING GOD'S PRESENCE
(Today with God)

What To Do With The New You

1. I remind myself — God is always present and active in my life and circumstances — whether I feel Him or not.
2. I am planning on looking for and recognizing God's presence in what   happens today.
3. God is protecting me in this moment, so I will be safe in Him today.
4. The enemy is trying to tell me I must be afraid. This is a lie!
5. When Jesus said, "Fear not" He meant He will take care of it.
6. When I fail, I can always start again right away.
7. I am becoming a more loving and serving person.
8. My love for God goes up and down. His love for me is always at peak intensity.
9. When God seems absent, it does not mean He is not there. It means He wants me to want Him.
10. God is intensely interested in every aspect of my life — relationships — work — hobbies — activities.
11. My way of experiencing God's presence will not be exactly like any other person's experience.
12. I am learning how to surrecder to God instead of struggling and straining so much.

~~~~~~~~~~~~

"Quiet Time"

Philippians 4:6 & 7

"Do not worry over anything whatever but instead pray — giving God every problem or trouble — with thanksgiving and the peace of God will keep constant guard over your hearts and minds ... as they rest in Christ Jesus." AMEN

LETTERS FROM GOD
(adapted from the Scriptures by Dick Lowey)
TO:_____ *(insert your name)* _____
–my adopted child
SUBJECT: Today
REFERENCE: Living with Me!
Dear Chosen One,

This is God speaking! I am NOT mad at you in any way today. I have made you the righteousness of God! (2 Corinthians 5:21) See yourself this way today.

Please note:

TODAY — I will be handling all your problems for you. I do not need your help. But I may ask for your cooperation at times. I love you and will show it in many ways today.

When you encounter a situation you cannot handle, please, don't attempt to solve it by yourself. Just put it into My *"Casting all your Cares"* box.

I will get to it — in My time — not yours. All situations will be resolved, but in My time. Once the matter is placed in My *"Casting all your Cares"* box — under My name, don't take it back into your own hands. And don't worry about it either — instead focus on all the blessings in your life.

Thank Me.

And by your own decision, have a nice day! (You only get so many of them, you know).

<u>I love you. And I will take care of you!</u> (Proverbs 3:5&6)

You are in My Grip—Forever !
GOD

Chapter 8.

"SPEAKING TO THE MOUNTAIN"

Often Christian believers overlook the concept in Scripture of opening our mouths and speaking to situations and circumstances. In Matthew's Gospel, Chapter 17: 20 and following, Jesus is explaining why the disciples could not cure an epileptic boy. He first rebukes them for their "unbelief" and then proceeds to heal the boy.

Jesus then explains to them about having faith the size of a mustard seed (very small) will enable the healer to "tell the mountain to move and it will move!"

This event teaches us that we must not only believe, but speak to the problem for God's power to be released.

What we often forget is that even the entrance of salvation — believing on Jesus — initially, for the first time, includes the process of "speaking out loud".

In Romans 10:9 &10 we read: *"If you confess with your mouth the Lord Jesus and believe in your heart that God has raised Him for the dead, you will be saved. For with the heart one believes unto righteousness and with the mouth confession is made unto salvation."*

Psalm 107:2 says: *"Let the redeemed of the Lord say so...whom He has redeemed from the hand of the enemy."*

I believe it is important for new believers to, early on, get into the practice of what I call "recital" — speaking Bible verses out loud (often in unison with other believers). I have seen in many instances that this procedure firmly plants God's Truth into the brains of young ones in the Lord.

We often close our Bible Study times by reciting out loud, together, the following verses which I have paraphrased:

1 John 5:11-13: *"This is the record — the witness — the dependable message — that God has given to us eternal, everlasting life, and this life is in His dynamic, powerful Son. He who personally receives the Son has this life, and he who does not receive the son, does not have this life. I write this message to you that you may be absolutely certain that you possess eternal life!"*

1 Corinthians 10:13: *"There is no trial or test or difficulty different from what other people experience, but God is faithful to you. He will not allow you to endure any problem which is beyond your ability, with God's help, to bear up under — He promises to provide a way out — an escape — a way to break free — a*

previously hidden or unknown door or gate so that you may be able to endure it."

John 1:12: *"Yet, to those who have received, believed on His name — have taken refuge in Him — are counting on Him — to them gave He the right — the qualifications necessary — to become and grow up as the children — the offspring — the heirs of God."*

Ephesians 2:8-10: *"For it is by Grace — God's unmerited favor — you have been saved — forgiven of all your sins — past — present — and future, through faith and that–not of yourselves — it is the gift of God — not by works of the flesh or self effort — leaving no room for human boasting — for we are God's masterpiece — created in Christ Jesus to find and perform those good works God prepared for us to do before the creation of the world!"*

Chapter 9.

"YOUR FOREVER FAMILY"

THE BODY OF CHRIST — THE CHURCH UNIVERSAL

God loves "community". He loves family! Indeed, God, Himself, IS a Community — a Family. He exists as one God in three Persons: Father — Son — Holy Spirit.

When God called Abraham in Genesis 12:1-3, He called Him away from His country — his family — 'his father's house" — to a new land that God would show him. God also promised him that he would become (bring forth) a Great Nation — fame and blessing would be his, and those who blessed him would be blessed, and those who cursed him would be cursed.

(Please note: When we bring others to Christ — we are — with God — starting, or further establishing churches or families on the earth.)

"Your Forever Family"

God's people — the Jews — have always considered themselves "family". Sometimes calling it a 'house" like "The House of David" or "The House of Israel". God's most recent formation is the "Body of Christ" — consisting of both Jews and Gentiles.

This is the new "Forever Family" — The Church Universal. (The word "Catholic" means universal, so it cannot be limited to Roman Catholics.)

It is of utmost importance that a young, new, believer meet together with other believers (Hebrews 10:24 & 25) for Worship, Fellowship, and the love shared together. Our witness depends on loving each other. Jesus says in John 13:35: *"By this shall all men know that you are My disciples, if you love one another."*

A basic definition of a church is: "The Gathering of those who believe in The Apostle's Creed."

The Apostle's Creed:
I believe in God the Father Almighty,
Maker of heaven and earth
And in Jesus Christ, His only Son
Who was conceived by the Holy Spirit,
Born of the virgin Mary,
Suffered under Pontious Pilate,
He was crucified, dead and buried.
He descended into hell
On the third day He rose from the dead
And ascended into heaven,
From thence He shall come again
And judge the living and the dead.
I believe in the Holy Catholic Church,

**The forgiveness of sins,
And the life everlasting. AMEN**

IMPORTANT NOTE:
(This creed represents basic, universal, beliefs of the early church — Christians in the first century)

Older, more mature believers can help the new ones find and bond with a community of worshipers, who will provide what is called for.

REMEMBER:
It is CHRISTIANITY — not "Churchianity" !
It is CHRISTIANITY — not "Holy-Spiritianity" !
It is CHRISTIANITY — not even rigid "Biblianty" !

Meaning: Beware of letting anything else be the Center of your life — but The Lord Jesus Christ!

Chapter 10

THE FOUR WILLS OF GOD

Before beginning this chapter a disclaimer is needed. In many ways this chapter is not the last chapter in the book. It is the first chapter in a second book. Why is that? Because the teaching in this chapter takes more maturity and grounding in the fundamentals of the faith. This chapter deals with the problem of evil and evil's relationship to God. Theologians have wrestled with this problem for thousands of years without coming up with a definitive solution. The following is my best attempt at making sense of the problem as I have interpreted the scriptures along with reading and dialoging with numerous people of God who are much wiser than I am. I also think that if God had wanted us to completely answer the problem of evil, He would know that we run the risk of the temptation of Adam & Eve all over again. That is that we would know the answer and could come to believe that we now have no need of Him. Thus, the Lord leaves us with a mystery, only catching glimpses of His workings. Paul catches this dilemma when he writes in 1 Corinthians 13:12 that, "Now we see but a poor reflection as in a mirror; then we shall see face to face. Now I know in part, then I shall know fully, even as I am fully known." (NIV).

Therefore, pray and watch for the right time when your student/disciple/mentee might be ready to dig into this material without it confusing or troubling them too much. I have written this chapter the way it is, on purpose, because it is more in line with the purpose & direction of this book; which is to present you with what I believe are some core & essential foundational truths. Then I move toward giving you a few directions (themes, scripture passages) and send you both off to dig in and explore the scriptures for yourselves & with each other.

The Four Wills of God help to explain or make sense of the **Problem of Evil**. The problem put in question form reads like this:

How can evil exist if God is totally good and God is all powerful?
Either God is not totally good and therefore lets evil exist (or causes evil).
or
God is not all powerful (less than omnipotent) And therefore cannot help but let evil exist.

What follows next are several, but not all, key passages of scripture for both of you to wrestle with. My hope and prayer is that you will begin to arrive at your own provisional conclusions through wrestling with the scriptures directly and allow them to inform you. While I have intentionally not added my own provisional conclusions, I have offered you some guidance in the form of some 'points to ponder'. Beyond that, you are on your own, so dive in and enjoy the journey.

Key Study #1
Genesis 2:1-17: The Original Temptation
Genesis 3: 1-24: The Fall of Human Beings into Sin
Points to Ponder:
1.) In Genesis 2:9 it says that the 'Tempting Tree' along with the 'Tree of Life' was placed in the middle of the Garden. Was this so that the 'Tempting Tree' would be visible to Adam Eve? Would it be accurate to say that God, in His omniscience (all knowing) as well as in his foreknowledge, must have known, ahead of time, that the first couple would sin, that is eat of the forbidden fruit? While God's foreknowledge does not excuse the 'Sin', might not this give an indication that even Adam & Eve's eating of the fruit was a part of God's plan?

2.) Why did the fruit represent 'The Knowledge of Good and Evil? A well known Presbyterian scholar puts it this way, " 'Knowing Good & Evil' is a description of 'not needing God' or 'running your own show'. Also 'Knowing Good and Evil' speaks of living by the

Law which is an Old Covenant Principle. Depending on 'Works' to justify your acceptance with God. Or, as it states elsewhere in Scripture, 'Everyone did what was right in their own eyes' (Judges 21:25). S the Fall was a fall into self-sufficiency. Genesis 3:22 states that the result of Adam and Eve's Sin was becoming like God (Knowing Good and Evil. The basic Sin of Satan is found in Isaiah 14:14, 'I will be like (take the place of) The Most High."

Key Study #2
Isaiah 45:5-7: God the Source of Tragedy?
Point to Ponder:

1.) ' I form Light and create Darkness; I bring peace and create calamity (Evil). The Lord does all these things.' Here God is the One creating all situations and Theologians have had problems with this passage of scripture for centuries. In Hebrew the word that is used here is 'Bara'. This is the same word that is used in Genesis 1 for 'Creates'. To get a better understanding of what is means, think of a child playing in the sand in a garden and allowing the sand to form itself into the shapes and patterns that come about. In a sense, when creation began, God was somewhat like the child in the garden allowing what was to be the 'creation' form itself into its prescribed pattern.

In Isaiah 45:7, God creates (Bara) and steps back and allows evil to come about. We now have what I have chosen to call the 'Permissive Will of God'. We can see an example of what I am trying to explain in the Book of Job where it seems to say that Satan must get 'permission' from God in order to torment Job (see Job 1:6 & Job 2:1-6). I also believe that before God allowed evil to exist, 'real love' had to have come into existance in the Garden. For without another option, that of Evil, humans had no real choice before them, and therefore they could not possibly fulfill God's desire to be 'freely chosen'. God is a God who wants to be wanted.

What do you think about the ideas presented here?

Key Study #3
Job 2:9-10: Job and his wife.

Job clearly states that God is involved in allowing adversity or trouble to happen. Job is commended for accepting adversity as coming, in some sense, from God.

What are your reactions to what Job seems to believe? In what ways does this belief square with your own beliefs about 'trouble'? Or not!

Key Study #4
1 Samuel 18: 6-11: God's Evil Spirit.

The scripture reads as follows. *"And it happened on the next day an evil ('Rah') spirit sent from God came upon Saul...."* The Hebrew word 'Rah' that is used here to mean evil actually means 'broken' or 'split' (possibly meaning schizophrenic). Nevertheless, God sent the spirit or as I like to put it, "God 'allowed' it for His purposes. " Consider this example. Often in Israel's courts, a person could be held responsible for a crime they did not directly commit, but only observed and did nothing to stop the crime. Is God, in this way, responsible for the presence of evil? What God does directly is Good because God is Good, right? What about what God does indirectly. Is that still Good? Yet is the following also true when C.S. Lewis says, "God values freedom as higher than obedience"? In what ways does what Lewis says fit with what has been presented before in the scripture. Or does it fit?

<u>Key Study #5</u>
<u>John 9: 1-7: The man who was born blind.</u>

"Now as Jesus passed by, He saw a man who was blind from birth and his disciples asked Him, 'Rabbi, who sinned, this man or his parents that he was born blind?' Jesus answered, ' Neither this man nor his parents sinned, but that the works of God might be revealed in him. I must work the works of Him who sent me while it is day.; the night is coming when no one can work. As long as I am in the world, I am the Light of the World.' Now when He had said these things, He spat

on the ground, and made clay with the saliva, and He anointed the eyes of the blind man with the clay and He said to him, 'Go wash in the pool of Siloam (which means sent).' So he went and washed and came back seeing."

From this event, do you think it is possible and accurate to conclude that Jesus saw this man's problem as an opportunity to show show or demonstrate the works of God? Might this passage offer us at least one reason that God allows evil to occur? Wouldn't that reason be that we are meant to be 'over comers'?

After the last Northern California earthquakes happened, there was very little looting. In fact, Californians were helping each other in many ways. For example, a nun was asked by a T.V. reporter, "In all of this misery, where is your God?" The nun immediately answered, "God is right here! Californians are learning to love each other." So often we only see the negative side of events. When, in reality, God is giving us ready-made opportunities to do good and helpful things for others, if only we have the 'eyes to see and the ears to hear', don't you think?

I will bring the section on key studies to a close by proposing that there are 'Four Wills of God' and Key Study #5 addresses the second Will of God which allows for 'love to exist. This second will of God, the Permissive Will of God is manifest all over the world. This seems to explain, to a great degree, why there is so much evil, don't you think? Now, pay attention to my words, Evil will only last for a predetermined period of time and then the Interventional Will of God will activate. Perhaps, shortly after that time, we might experience the Final Will of God which marks the end of the ages and God's bringing everything back together, setting everything right again with Him reigning supreme! What do make of that? What do you think about that?

Possible Study Questions

1. **Job's friends thought that there must have been sin in Job's life for him to be enduring so much suffering. What do you understand is the perspective that leads Job's friends to think this way?**
2. **What do you think is behind the disciples asking Jesus why this man was born blind?**
3. **Describe Jesus' reason for this happening to the blind man.**
4. **When you encounter tragedy in life, what does this story tell you to do?**
5. **Describe, in your own words, what you think the relationship is between sin and tragic circumstances. Describe what leads you to think that way.**
6. **In what ways does seeing tragedy as an opportunity to do good affect your thinking about evil and the place of evil?**
7. **What do you think about the fact that 'over coming' seems so important to God?**

8. Give some examples, both general and personal, of negative events bringing about a good outcome.
9. In what ways does the idea of 'negative events bringing about a good outcome fit with Romans 8:28?

Many Christians are reluctant to hold God responsible, in any way, for the existence of evil and tragedy. They are, somewhat glibly, apt to say something like, "Evil is Satan's doing! Don't blame God for it!" The problem with this kind of thinking is that it reflects a hidden philosophy, that of 'Dualism'.

Dualism, as used in this case, describes a split world where **Good** is represented by God and **Evil** is represented by Satan. Dualism implies that these two Gods are equal in power and stature. It diagrams like this:

<u>God</u>   &   <u>Satan</u>
Good   Evil

Two Gods?
No!!!
Remember Israel's monotheistic refrain from Isaiah 45:5
'Hear, O Israel. The Lord God is one God.'

The Four Wills of God are helpful in solving the dilemma of Dualism. The 2nd Will of God speaks to us that evil is no surprise to a Sovereign God. Evil exists because God permits evil to exist. Evil exists to serve

God purposes, which we mostly experience in mystery & paradox. The Four Wills of God are described as follows.

The Four Wills of God

1. **<u>The Initial or Original Will of God</u>**

   One might call this, God's creational Will. This will includes the reality that God desires us to want to choose to love Him back. This desire cannot take place without human kind having free will. Free will implies that there are at least two choices.

   Therefore, there must be an option not to freely choose to love & trust God. Thus, the need for evil.

2. **<u>The Permissive Will of God</u>**

   The creation of Lucifer and his decision, without being tempted, to seek to be 'like' (the same as) God. Lucifer then tempted & took 1/3 of the angels with him when fell out of heaven. Lucifer then (was allowed?) to tempt Adam & Eve. Through them humankind fell and all future humans with them. Thus we have the heredity of sin within us. Through this an alternative to God is provided and love is now possible.

3. **<u>The Interventional Will of God</u>**

   God begins His radical restoration of humankind, along with all of Creation (which contains another whole doctrinal investigation), through the life, death, resurrection, and ascension of Christ.

4. **<u>The Ultimate or Final Will of God</u>**
This will is marked by the return of Jesus as King who casts Lucifer down forever, ends, once and for all, all tears & suffering, finishes off the old creation, ushers in the new creation in the form of the 'new heaven and the new earth coming down from heaven with Jesus Christ the Lord sitting on the throne and ruling forever.

Wow!

It kind of takes your breath away doesn't it.

BIBLIOGRAPHY

Know What you Believe - By Paul Little

What the Bible is All About - By Henrietta C. Mears

Unmerited Favor - By Joseph Prince

How to Be a Christian Without Being Religious - By Fritz Ridinour

Sit, Walk, Stand - By Watchman Nee

My Heart, Christ's Home - By Robert Munger

The Mark of the Christian - By Francis Schaffer

CPSIA information can be obtained at www.ICGtesting.com
Printed in the USA
BVOW05s0122031214

377448BV00001B/14/P

9 781498 417235